DISCUSSION GUIDE

silverlining

a life application journey through the dynamics of grief

DR. T. DAVID WILLETS

Silverlining Discussion Guide
© 2013 by Dr. T. David Willets

Published by Insight International
4739 E. 91st Street, Suite 210
Tulsa, OK 74137
918-493-1718

ISBN: 978-1-890900-88-5

Printed in the United States of America

This Discussion Guide is designed to facilitate
interaction in a small group setting
with the print version
and video series of *Silverlining*.

Life Principle

*"Rejoice with those who rejoice;
mourn with those who mourn."*

Romans 12:15

CONTENTS

My Story

On May 4, 2004, my wife of 27 years and 18-year-old daughter came by my office to say good-bye as they were leaving on an exciting trip. At that time, I was senior pastor of a church in Louisiana. That was the last time I saw them alive. They were on their way to visit the campus of a private university in Oklahoma where my daughter was to audition for a talent-ship in acting. Around 3:30 in the afternoon, as they were driving on a turnpike, we were speaking via cell phone when my wife said, "I'd better get off, now. It's starting to rain." In the background my daughter shouted, "I love you, Daddy." That was the last time I spoke with them.

Around 7:00 that evening the doorbell rang at my home. Two Louisiana state highway patrol officers were at my door. One of them said to me, "There has been a car accident." At that split moment, my mind assumed the accident involved someone in the church I was serving. The officer handed me a teletype that read, "Approximately 4:05 p.m. The Oklahoma Indian Nations Turnpike, northbound by exit 69. Two fatalities. Leesa L. Willets and Lauryn K. Willets." I paused and read it again. Then I said in astonishment, "They're dead?"

From that moment until this present moment, my life has changed. While the crushing blow of agonizing pain became my meat and drink for days and weeks following the reading of that teletype, I have discovered more silver linings to that storm than I ever thought possible. This video series and Discussion Guide package is just one of them. Open your heart as you embark on your journey toward healing through the dynamics of grief.

What is Your Significant Loss?

On this one page, write a narrative describing the event(s) that has placed you on the journey of grief. Be as open as you feel comfortable at this time.

Share Your Story

If you are ready to do so, read the one-page description of your significant loss. This small group is set in a "judgment-free zone." Your loss is significant to you, and that is all that matters.

Please reserve any comments or discussion on each story during this step. This Discussion Guide is designed to facilitate those activities along the way. Just share your story.

SESSION 1

"Why Did This Happen to Me?"

The two men who built their houses by the river were different from one another in the methods they used for construction. But is there any reason to believe that one man deserved the flooding rain to come more than the other?

No it rains on everyone

Although some people may not say it, they think there must be a reason why a significant loss has come to your life. While they have no factual reason to think that, they do anyway. Do people do that because of superstition or because they think there might be a curse on you or what?

The Bible says, *"It rains on good people and bad people alike."* (See Matthew 5:45.) In this session Dr. Willets talks about a "justice meter" built into every person. Mark on the justice meter below where your feelings register in your particular loss. The farther you mark on the right side of the meter indicates you feel your loss is the most "unfair."

Discuss where you are on the "justice meter."

_____

_____

_____

_____

_____

_____

_____

_____

_____

_____

The Law of Cause and Effect says there is a direct connection between your significant loss and something you have done or not done. Is there a factual reason to believe your significant loss is rooted in the Law of Cause and Effect? If "yes," what is the specific correlation? If "no," do you still <u>feel</u> that there is?

_____

_____

_____

_____

_____

_____

Grief comes to us when we have experienced a significant loss, and the "significance" of our loss is solely defined by our emotions, not by what others may call "valuable."

From your personal perspective, share with the group the great value of your significant loss.

_____

_____

_____

_____

_____

_____

_____

_____

Let's Lay Down the Wrestling Mat!

You may or may not be a "spiritual" person. You may not even believe in God. However, for the sake that you might find an answer to the question, "Why did this happen to me?" please consider participating in this next step.

Dr. Willets mentions four spiritual principles that can be used as a mat on which you and God can wrestle through this most difficult question in the grieving process. They are:

- God knows everything.
- We don't know everything.
- God is always working things out for our good.
- My best option is to trust God.

God Knows Everything

All the main religions of the world – Christianity, Judaism, Islam and Hinduism – believe in this theological concept explaining the extent to what God knows: God is _____.

Discuss how it makes you feel, in light of your significant loss, that God knows every detail of your past, present and future life. There are no wrong or bad emotions in this discussion, just honesty.

_____

_____

_____

_____

_____

_____

_____

We Don't Know Everything

This doesn't mean we don't know anything, we just don't know everything! Take a few minutes and use this principle to become more acquainted with the people in your group. Each of you think of a topic you know quite a bit about. It may be your work profession or a hobby or some specific area of interest. Share with each other what that one topic is and, generally, what you know about it.

_____

_____

_____

_____

_____

Surprising, isn't it? You didn't know that much about all the topics mentioned, did you? Think about how much more we don't know.

God Is Always Working Things Out for Our Good

Ask someone in the group to use their cell phone or smart pad and go to www.biblegateway.com. Once there, search for Romans 8:28. Read that verse to see where Dr. Willets gets this life principle.

Discuss these questions:

- Does this principle state that all things are good that happen to us?

  _____

  _____

  _____

  _____

  _____

  _____

  _____

- Is it possible for you to "love God" and still have strong negative emotions toward Him? Can a parent love her child and still have strong negative emotions toward him/her?

  _____

  _____

  _____

  _____

  _____

  _____

- Most people believe that God has a purpose for everything. It might not be possible to see it right now, but can you allow the thought that God has a purpose for your life through your significant loss?

  _____

  _____

  _____

  _____

  _____

  _____

My Best Option Is to Trust God

When asking the question, "Why did this happen to me?" you have the option of trying to figure it out on your own. But why would you do that when you don't know everything, but God does know everything and He is working in ways you cannot see to bring good out of your painful loss?

Can you think of a time when your parents or caregivers did something for your good, but you didn't like or understand it? Maybe you've had that experience as a parent with your child. Take a few moments and discuss that experience with the group.

_____

_____

_____

_____

_____

_____

Is there someone in the group who can share something good that has come out of your painful loss?

_____

_____

_____

_____

_____

_____

_____

_____

There is an old saying that goes, "Difficulties in life can make you either bitter or better." It may be just too hard to see right now, but can you think of something that might make you better because of your significant loss?

_____

_____

_____

_____

_____

_____

_____

_____

_____

_____

_____

_____

_____

_____

_____

_____

_____

_____

_____

_____

There Are Different Types of Storms

As silly as it is to say, "There is only one type of storm on Mother Nature's menu," it is equally ridiculous to say, "There is only one reason a person experiences grief – the death of a loved one." We grieve when something or someone significant to us has died. In the case of losing something, death means "the ending of."

If we don't deal with the death of those things that are significant to us, we will suffer from a terminal case of sadness. The intensity of grieving these losses will vary according the significance we place on them.

You may have joined this group because something significant to you has died. The group acknowledges the significance of your loss and that your pain is real. Each member is here to support you.

Take a few moments as a group and share some experiences of losing something (not someone) significant to you that caused you real grief.

You Have to Face the Grief Monster

The grief monster is that emotional pain you feel when the death of whatever you are grieving is triggered in your mind. Can you describe to the group how you initially start to feel when the grief monster begins knocking at your emotional door?

_____

_____

_____

_____

_____

Can you share with the group some of the triggers you've experienced that have caused the grief monster to knock at your emotional door? There may be several triggers.

_____

_____

_____

_____

_____

How do you typically respond when the grief monster starts to knock?

_____

_____

_____

_____

People may be well-intentioned, but many times they give us harmful advice on how to avoid the grief monster, such as, "When you get that feeling coming on, give me a call and we'll go play golf." People who care for you don't want to see you in pain. That's why they say such things. However, if you don't open your emotional door and wrestle it out with the grief monster, your pain will turn into anger, bitterness and resentment.

If you feel comfortable doing so, share with the group what it's like when you wrestle with the grief monster.

_____

_____

_____

_____

How do you feel when your wrestling sessions with the grief monster are over?

_____

_____

_____

_____

_____

_____

_____

_____

The grief monster will come knocking less often, over time, if you face him down. In the past few weeks, how many times have you opened the door to the grief monster and wrestled it out with him?

_____

_____

_____

_____

_____

"My Storm Changes from Hail to Rain to Wind"

Your grief journey is a process, not a one-time event where you feel intense pain, then you go back to "normal." Perhaps you've heard that there are stages in the grieving process. It's true. Dr. Willets states that there are four general stages in the grieving process: trauma, disorientation, adjustment and rebuilding. There is a multitude of emotions we feel during each of these stages.

If you are able to do so, share with the group how you felt when you first learned of the trauma that hurled you into grief.

_____

_____

_____

_____

_____

_____

_____

_____

You may have joined this group during the trauma stage of your grief. We know your pain is intense, and we are here to support you through it.

Is there anyone(s) in the group who can describe your emotions during the disorientation stage of the grieving process?

_____

_____

_____

_____

During the adjustment stage of the grieving process, you wrestle less with the grief monster (emotional meltdown) and gain some perspective on the reality of your loss. While the variety and intensity of emotions still come in this stage, you begin to have the ability to feel more comfortable with people, places, traditions and activities in your life.

Your life may be far from the "new normal" you hope to experience, but you are not as emotionally overwhelmed as you were during the trauma and disorientation stages.

Perhaps someone in this group might consider themselves in the adjustment stage of grief. Would you be willing to share what you are experiencing in this stage?

_____

_____

_____

_____

_____

_____

_____

One of the most common mistakes we make during the grieving process is to tell ourselves we have "worked through" a particular stage, as if we will never deal with the intense emotions of that stage again. But that is not true.

In the grieving process, our emotions can dramatically change with our circumstances. This dynamic may leave people discouraged when they experience the raw emotions of any earlier stage while deep into the process of a later stage. They feel they are "going backwards." But remember, grieving is a process not a procedure.

Would someone(s) in the group who has experienced this dynamic be willing to share what happened to them?

_____

_____

_____

_____

_____

_____

The death of a child is unique among all the losses one can experience in life. This topic is addressed in the print version of *Silverlining*. You may secure a copy through www.silverlining.ws.

If there is someone(s) in this group who has experienced the death of a beloved child, would you be willing to share what that is like for you? If you are not comfortable in doing so, the group respects your privacy and supports you completely.

_____

_____

_____

_____

_____

_____

_____

Few people experience the height, depth and width of human emotions like those who have been deeply hurt by the death of someone or something significant. They tend to have more "soul." The infliction brought on by a significant death pierces into the core, the soul. When your soul has been bruised, life is never the same.

Have you felt any new emotions as you have been on your grief journey? There are no bad emotions, so please be vulnerable with the group and open your soul.

_____

_____

_____

_____

_____

_____

_____

A significant loss will expand and intensify the range of emotions you have felt all your life. Have you found that to be true in your experience? Would you share some examples with the group?

_____

_____

_____

_____

_____

_____

_____

_____

Through the grief journey, the discovery of new emotions and intensification of existing emotions can create in us what Dr. Willets calls "soulishness." Becoming *soulish* can be a wonderful gift.

Is there anyone(s) in the group who is experiencing this gift and can describe it?

_____

_____

_____

_____

_____

_____

_____

_____

Do you know someone who has the gift of soulishness? My guess is he/she has experienced some significant losses in their life. A helpful exercise for you would be to spend some time talking with them. Ask them how they grew emotionally and spiritually through the pain of their loss.

At some point, while this group is meeting, you may want to share with them what you learned from this exercise.

One Rainbow Size Does Not Fit All

A rainbow is such a beautiful image of hope. At this point on your grief journey, your emotional rainbow is starting to form. Is there someone(s) in the group who can describe the season in your grief journey when the clouds of your particular storm began to break and you caught a glimpse of a rainbow appearing in your life?

_____

_____

_____

_____

_____

_____

We have already established that every person grieves in his or her own unique way. That is also true of *how long* a person grieves until he or she feels a "new normal" for them has arrived.

Community mores and unspoken "rules" too often dictate how and how long a person should grieve. These communities include family, friends and religious groups. Even various regions of the country have different expectations for a grieving person. What are some of those expectations in your personal communities?

_____

_____

_____

_____

_____

_____

_____

_____

_____

Discuss why you should keep your emotional eyes wide open during the first year of your grief journey.

_____

_____

_____

_____

_____

_____

_____

_____

Is there someone(s) in the group who is willing to tell about a conflict in community expectations and your personal readiness to move forward in your grief process?

_____

_____

_____

_____

_____

_____

_____

_____

_____

_____

There are a number of good reasons you are participating in this small group, not the least of which is bonding with some fellow soul-travelers on the journey of grief.

An enjoyable way to bond with someone is to watch a good movie together. Here's a suggestion: Pick a movie that deals with the topics of love, loss and grief. A few recommendations are listed below. Choose a night when all or most of you in the group can attend. Perhaps someone in the group would volunteer your home to watch the movie together. Get some popcorn and enjoy the movie!

At the conclusion of the movie, take a few minutes and discuss the dynamics of grief you can identify. Some of the characters in the movie will model healthy grief and others will model harmful grief.

A River Runs Through It

On Golden Pond

Ordinary People

Of course, there are other good movies that deal with the topics of love, loss and grief. You may find one that is more agreeable to the group.

Preparing for the Next Storm

Return to chapter one in your Discussion Guide and review your answer to the first question about the two men who built their houses by the banks of a river.

As a backdrop to this session's discussion, remember this life principle: "The way you make it through a traumatic event depends on what you believe going into the event." With that in mind, let's attempt to build a belief system that will withstand the emotional blows of any storm that may come your way.

A Spiritual Foundation

You may or may not consider yourself to be a "religious" person. This discussion is not an attempt to manipulate you into joining any organized religion. Interestingly, however, the only time the word "religion" is mentioned in the New Testament of the Bible is found in the context of those who are struggling because of a significant loss. It is found in James 1:27: *"Religion that God our Father accepts as pure and faultless is this: to look after orphans and widows in their distress...."*

Perhaps the reason so many people don't identify themselves as "religious" is because so many religious communities have not adhered to the admonition above. Understandable.

A spiritual foundation is a set of beliefs that guide the way you live your everyday life. A spiritual foundation answers the question, in some way, "Does death end it all?" A spiritual foundation offers a response to the human dilemma of pain and suffering.

Take some time to discuss this vital question as you build your spiritual foundation; "Does what I believe spiritually give me comfort and a basis of hope when the storms of life hit?"

_____

_____

_____

_____

_____

_____

_____

_____

_____

_____

_____

_____

_____

_____

_____

You may find it helpful in building your spiritual foundation to see what sustained Dr. Willets through the trauma and grief of losing his wife and daughter. You will find those beliefs at www.silverlining.ws. Click on the link, "About Dr. Willets."

Building the Superstructure of Your Beliefs

The superstructure of a building is the skeleton that holds everything together above the foundation. These are the heavy beams and load-bearing walls. A strong belief system also has a sturdy superstructure that rests on the foundation.

You determine the superstructure of your beliefs by clearly identifying what is truly significant and valuable to you. These are the people and things that have your full devotion. Give this step some serious thought. You are creating a list of "most" significant and valuable people and/or things in your life. You may declare no more than five categories with specific names and/or areas that define that category.

For example: My immediate family (Jane, Jake and Joey). My extended family (only the names of those whom you are willing to give your full devotion. This does not mean you don't appreciate others in your extended family, but your uncle in Des Moines and your cousin in Dallas are not on your "most" list).

1. _____

_____

_____

2. _____

_____

_____

3. _____

_____

_____

4. _____

_____

_____

5. _____

_____

_____

Why is this exercise necessary? There are two primary reasons: First, this list will help define where you will invest your time, energy and resources. Second, this list may limit the number of deep grief events in your life. While we grieve all losses with differing intensities, this "most" list will help you be prepared for any level of loss in a particular category in the future.

Completing the Structural Elements of Your Beliefs

If a building only has a foundation and superstructure, it won't be very functional. Next, construct the inner and outer walls of your life with purpose and meaning. Generally speaking, people who are focused on a specific purpose and meaningful activities in life are far more fulfilled than those who aren't. This is a wonderful opportunity for you to find a beautiful silver lining to your storm.

Discuss with the group these questions: "What one thing have I truly had a passion for in life?" "Is there something I've learned or am learning through this grief process that can be a potential driver for meaning in my life?" Please be transparent.

_____

_____

_____

_____

_____

_____

_____

_____

_____

Perhaps the group can offer some practical suggestions on how you can build your passion into your daily life.

_____

_____

_____

_____

_____

_____

Identify Your Core Support Group

Someone said, "The difference between you and Fido is that you put pictures on the walls of your house and he doesn't in his doghouse." Once the foundation, superstructure and structure of your belief system have been built, adorn your life with a core support group.

A core support group is composed of no more than three people you can count on to share the deepest lows of your life, at any time of the day and night. These are the people who will show up for you at three o'clock in the morning. If you already have three of these people in your life, consider yourself to be extremely blessed. Most people might have one.

Take a few minutes and write down the names of people who might be candidates for your core support group. Remember, to have this kind of friend you must be this kind of friend.

_____

_____

_____

_____

_____

_____

_____

Now, choose only three.

_____

_____

_____

Make sure you take time to explain your expectations to these three people. Don't assume they fully understand what it means to be a three o'clock in the morning friend.

CONTACT DR. WILLETS

www.silverlining.ws

david@silverlining.ws

Postal mail:

4739 East 5th Street, Tulsa, OK 74112

Silverlining is an outreach of Numa Ministries, Inc.

CPSIA information can be obtained
at www.ICGtesting.com
Printed in the USA
FFOW05n0327270115

9 781890 900885